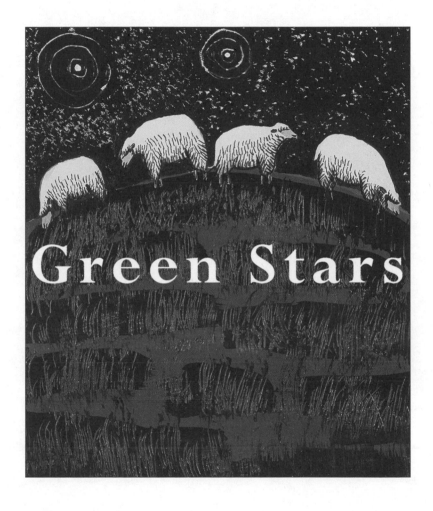

Green Stars

Green Stars

Poems

To VIVIAN —
I hope to see you
this summer.
CHM,
warmly
Charlotte

Charlotte Hilary Matthews

Iris Press
Oak Ridge, Tennessee

Library of Congress Cataloging-in-Publication Data

Matthews, Charlotte Hilary, 1966-
Green stars : poems / Charlotte Hilary Matthews.
  p. cm.
ISBN-13: 978-0-916078-63-8
ISBN-13: 978-0-916078-64-5 (pbk. : alk. paper)
ISBN-10: 0-916078-63-9
ISBN-10: 0-916078-64-7 (pbk. : alk. paper)
I. Title.
PS3613.A8447G74 2005
811'.6—dc22

2005030598

Acknowledgments

Grateful acknowledgment is made to the following publications in which these poems first appeared.

Appalachian Journal: "Country Auction"
Borderlands: Texas Poetry Review: "Listening to the News Story" (as "Listening to the News")
Eclipse: "Letter," "A Study of Gratitude"
Mississippi Review: "Last Dream Before Waking," "The Feel of Water"
Meridian: "The Shape of Memory"
Paper Street Press: "Catalogue of Silence"
Poet Lore: "Growing Up in Washington"
Potomac Review: "Two Moments With Strangers"
Puddinghouse Farming Anthology: "Country Burial"
Sacred Bearings: "What We Watch Behind Glass"
Shade: "Bottom of the Ocean," "County Airstrip," "Daylight Savings Time," "Luminescence," "The Flat Track"
Sou'wester: "Survival Float," "December 7, 1941," "Magic Show"
Spoon River Poetry Review: "Augury"
Streetlight: "What the Snow Reveals"
Tar River Poetry: "After My Father Leaves"
Virginia Writing: "Person, House, Tree"

Because this book arises principally from memory, I extend my gratitude to those luminous people and places who are lit rooms in my mind: my brother Clark, the boxwood gardens of The Washington National Cathedral, Mary Lela and Ted Sherburne, the early morning creek at Turkey Run, Jennifer Davis, the Thorp cabin in Maine, Rebecca Hutchinson, 3111 Garfield Street, Langley Freeauf, Emma and Garland.

In memory of my mother

Joan Carson Matthews

The world has wonderful details
if you can just get it a little closer than usual.

—Annie Dower

Contents

I

II

III

Introductory Note

Green Stars introduces poet Charlotte Matthews as an extraordinary observer of details of the world, a celebrant of scent and sound and all they conjure back into our half-remembered selves. It is her breath and heart breaking task to remind us what makes us human. These are the remnants of family: the bells that ring from childhood and the love that scars even as it binds, never letting us go.

—Mary Chapin Carpenter

Poem in Fear of War

I am the girl in the garden
bent over rows of spring peas
hoping, unexplainably, that they have
not grown in the dark of night.
Earlier, out on the leaf pile,
six sparrows were singing
under their breath without mercy
as if nothing horrific has ever come to pass.

Clearly none of us wants to mention
how dangerous this could be.

Remember how in the Iliad
all the important decisions
were made by the gods,
leaving men free to shift about
the way Albert's cows do,
grouping in whatever
shade the sun has left behind.

I

O Flower, whose fragrance tender
   With sweetness fills the air,
   Dispel in glorious splendor
   The darkness everywhere.

—Rosa Mystica, 1599

Augury

What I want to know is why
each time I fall back asleep
my mother is still dying.
Usually she's sick
and I'm the only one
who knows
how bad it really is.
She tells me truths
she doesn't think
my brother can bear,
but this has gone on for years,
a marsh in which the haze
of late afternoon floats up
faint, unsolvable,
or the plough
my neighbor drives,
barely moving
in the June field.
Think of your toes, she told me.
Think of ironing
or conjugating a verb.
Think of anything
but this.

Each time the school bus stopped
in front of a house,
I saw the body of a parent
leaning down,
blinds still drawn
and the children inside
who didn't want to be picked up
or go away like I did.

This is exactly what I was afraid of,
and it keeps on happening.

The Feel of Water

At this moment in the rain, people are walking the last
blocks to work, their minds on the slick, dark streets
and the taxis who pace themselves to miss red lights.

When the sun comes out at noon, a woman will spend
her lunch break on the front steps of her building, cool marble
hard on her thighs. She will squint at the sky and remember
how her mother taught her to cross her legs,
one ankle draped over the other.

A student practices cello, notes dark
and hollow the way you would imagine the inside
of a cave or the house on the corner for sale so long
neighborhood children have broken into the backyard
and made a fort there, digging in mulch and magnolia leaves.

My mother gave me a cigar box after my brother
was born. Inside it a tiny filly so smooth the plastic
had the feel of water or green velvet on a girl's dress.
Because of my mother's honesty, I regard the moment
as a sort of exchange: this horse for this new boy.

Sometimes I dream the back field of our house goes
all the way to the river and my mother is still alive,
standing by her desk, arranging her day.

What Floats

My daughter's imaginary
friend is invisible
because she lives
in the light,
because she is
everywhere at once.

All afternoon at the bridge
we throw bread to the fish.
On the shallow water's surface
walnuts float,
their insides black and porous
as marrow. And yellow leaves
from the poplar
whose empty shells
click in the wind.
The creek bed's the color
of deer and of the painted
box turtle who retreats
into his shell so he can disappear.

The soul is like trust,
like a cloud whose shape of angel, or ox,
is exactly what we need it to be.

The Shape of Memory

At first it is hard to tell what they are,
grouped under shadowy trees,
or grazing in the cool dark
gauzy moon over Buck Mountain.
Driving home, I came upon a calf
in the creek road. He was minutes old, trying to stand,
his mother pacing the fence's other side
where he must have slid in the water of his birth.
It was February, the weather forgiving.
The calf was still wet, fur black as charcoal,
luminous in perfect whorls.
And when Mr. Hall came in his truck
to open the gate, he did not speak.
He stood watching a long time,
hands steady on the cold chain.
I remember how the distant line of spruce
looked grayer than ever before, the night
opened around us, coming out of the soft, dirt road.
But there are things I do not remember at all.
Sometimes it's only the still smell of a public hallway
or a voice over the radio, the way the words
are held in the speaker's mouth.
Summers, cleaning trout on the chipped wellhead,
we scraped our knives against the scales
until they came off thin, the grass
around us littered with flecks of silver light.
The wellhead is scarlet with fish blood.
Cattails click on the shore road.
My father is watching over me
in case I ever have to do this alone.

Survival Float

Because the sun is at just the right angle
I can see particles suspended,
bits of wood or leaf,
where we lie on our stomachs
learning to float,
learning to wait for rescue
as if some day we will be
far out in a vast body of water
with nothing to hold onto
and no one who knows where we are.

I imagine there will be days of waiting
in brown flecked water,
our legs dangling,
excessive and invisible beneath us.
We are wearing heavy clothes,
blue jeans and plaid flannel shirts we tie
at the waist and blow up
to keep us afloat longer,
the trapped air in our shirts ballooning.
We are twelve hunchbacks
coiled in murky water.

This is my mother's greatest fear:
being forgotten,
being overlooked or passed by.
As a child she hid
in the neighbor's backyard,
behind the pear tree,
hoping her mother
would notice she was gone.

Two Childhoods

It's night in the picture book
about the zookeeper who checks
with his flashlight the animals,
pausing in the shapeless dark
to account for them, thin new moon
draped overhead.
Emma tells me what is happening,
each time the story slightly
changes, the young wanting sleep
today, tired after a long time in the sun.
My brother and I take her
to the neighborhood where we grew up.
From the level of the sidewalk,
we look at the pale green shutters
of the rowhouse on 38th.
He points to the scar in the brick
where an icebox used to be.
Everything's the same, really, except
if you look in the windows.

Lately, I've wanted to be on a ferry,
closed in a glass compartment
above the ocean, sound
of seagulls hovering restless
over the bow, or asleep by myself
in an upstairs room
of the house where we lived.
It would be in secret, a summer
afternoon, blinds pulled
so the only light's hazy,
half-filtered, coming in
through the cracks.
Whenever I close my eyes,

the house is exactly the way
we left it. And the world outside
is quiet, waiting for us.

December 7, 1941

When the war came over the radio,
my mother, the youngest and at home,
heard the single words like trinkets
to collect, buttons portioned in flowered boxes,
and loved some, their feel on her tongue.
She must have heard the Sunday announcer
and thought it was the same as always,
the brief news. But then she must have understood
something in his voice, how he spoke more clearly.
Maybe her aunt kept the radio on for too long
and quietly set down her mending.
Or maybe she simply wondered
about the names, how they sounded.
Whatever it was, she held to the word
proudly naming her puppet Pearl.
Her father, hearing this, slapped her hard.

Listening to the News Story

They have found what they are looking for
the week my daughter learns to walk.
Longer than I can imagine archaeologists
have stared into their monitors hoping
for some pale, unremarkable object—
a shell worn dull from countless years
lying on the ocean floor—to prove
the salty Black Sea was once a small lake,
that there was a great flood after all.
This time, as the dredge clears the stern,
bits of freshwater mollusk fall
to the boat's shadowy hull.
They cheer, distant through the radio.
Emma holds both fists before her,
ballast for this trip.

Bottom of the Ocean

I want my mother to draw me a tall
house on a hill, or a kitchen
table, something solid
that can bear its own weight.

At night, after I'm in bed,
she goes to check the bees, lifting
the outer lid to watch them
asleep in their box beside the orchard.

So hot this May,
all afternoon the workers
have fanned their wings,
keeping the wax from melting.

Putting her face close
she smells the dim honey,
dreams she is young again,
in Berlin after the war.

The bees have become
so still she forgets
they are there, invisible
as kelp on the ocean floor.

In the morning when I ask her
for a rabbit, she draws one
from behind so we are looking
out at the exact same world.

Daylight Savings Time

Starting in late February my mother
would cut the weather page
out of the newspaper
and put it on the refrigerator
as a sign of hope: each day
a minute or two more light.

But it's autumn now.
This week the time changed,
and it's dark by six.
Think of it as temporary, I tell myself:
an alcove or loft, place
for waiting out of harm's way.

I take my daughter to dinner.
As we sit behind the plate glass
of Shoney's, the parking lot grows
appalling at the farthest edges.

County Airstrip

How long in that same fit I lay I have not to declare.
—Samuel Taylor Coleridge

Below, the world is reduced
like a stable set,
horses molded the size
of a half dollar,
and the ground tended,
shorn, a man waking
at dawn to watch over
hedgerows and fields
so perfect there must be
nothing to fear.
A Cessna's light weight
allows it to glide to safety
in case the engine fails,
air lifting the plane
as if on strings.

There is a river
and it has no sound at all.

A child dreams
deep blue wallpaper.
In it, birds in a marsh,
layer upon layer of color
so steeped around them they
will never have to leave.

I keep on telling this story,
can't get rid of it
no matter what.
Last weekend I drove
by my mother's house,

and it was okay.
I saw it was a fine house,
meaning it will last,
meaning there is something
left after all.

The Distinct Shadows of Winter

In another city my mother sits
in her plain kitchen, afternoon sun
shifting over worn linoleum squares.
I tell myself I can see her as she is, sitting alone,
holding her wishes tight to herself
the way you hold a piece of mending
so nothing falls or gets lost.

I tell her the things I have been keeping secret.
I tell her, but she cannot hear from so far away.

I put out food for the jays
who come from the locust on the fence line,
their feathers the insistent blue of slate.
I watch them from this window where yesterday
I saw light's changing, the way it moves
faster in winter and dusk.
I want to be able to say exactly how it looked,
how it lit the hill across the creek red,
stayed like that much longer than I expected.

My mother prides herself in being steady.
Faced with something difficult,
she takes to reading even more,
immersed in a mystery silently all night.
For years after my father died
we'd go to distant graveyards,
walking by names we didn't know,
that couldn't matter, noting the dates and ages
with a vague and brief half-interest.

If you hold a thing inside yourself too long it takes
on a life of its own until you cannot mention it again.

Victory Gardens

My mother was seven when we entered the war.
The tense expression on her father's face
altered him so, to her, the war took on
a sealed, unquestionable grandeur.

She told me this in the car
driving past tended plots at the foot
of an apartment building, earth gleaming black
with manure and lime from miles away.

We are walking in the city garden
between cabbages. Or I am pasting
tissue paper onto cardboard
making red and orange birds.

Across the hall she is at her desk
paying bills, venetian blinds half
closed so when cars pass
the room is striped with sudden light.

There are whole years grouped inside me.
I'll remember one moment only
to realize I must have been
older than I'd thought.

Sometimes, in winter, we go to a matinee.
Before the movie starts, in the dark theater,
I can smell the wool of her blazer so close,
rising as she breathes in the seat right next to me.

After My Father Leaves

She sits at the kitchen table smoking an L&M.
The first cool of evening pushes itself
into the gray flagstones of the backyard.
She is listening to the Saturday opera.
Upstairs I read as if nothing has happened.
It is early spring, the pond turns over
in silence, its dark underneath rising weightless.
I try to walk down the tall, carpeted stairs
to tell her it doesn't matter,
to tell her we weren't happy anyway,
but suddenly the house is quiet,
the opera over or turned off.

Nights We Came Home

Our house was, for those single nights, a place not part of us,
not swollen with memory: stain on the speaker
shaped like the anger that came after,
kitchen stove where my mother leaned
and told me what she really wanted:
to pack a small bag and go be someone else.

As a girl she spent her summers alone
in a high-ceilinged room, propping herself
on her elbows, reading all day, safe from the moving world.
Above her a gray fan filled the space
with steadiness. Sometimes, on the worn rug, she would turn
onto her back and stare at the tin above:
dashes and ovals she didn't yet know as egg and dart.

She still remembers those books.
She would tell me what happened
as I paced around and around her,
a mystery open on her lap,
the same Scott Joplin rag, false and cheerful,
playing for hours.

My Neighbor's Fear of Winter

What she tells me is about wood:
how hickory and locust are best
burning long and hot and slow.

Her voice is solemn like the very worst news.

The night he left she was at the window
hoping to see whose face was in the moon,
her breath a thin fog all around.

Until the outside air arranged itself in secrets.

Levels of the House

My mother is upstairs reading in her paisley chair.
Streetlights are coming on,
the ground moist with early spring.
I should go tell her it's time to move
downstairs, almost evening and dinner soon.
But there is something perfect about how she sits,
her book propped on a worn pillow, the room
growing dark without her knowing it.

This is where she always waited,
for my brother, or me, or my father—
even after he stopped coming home.
She was abiding, only the title
of the borrowed novel changing as she looked
up to listen to stories of where we'd been.

One August, just back from camp, I told her
how, on the last night, each of us placed
a lit candle in the river and watched it float far
out of sight down the Cacapon.
She looked to the side, then, and nodded.

Out in the alley, neighbors call their children
home, one by one, for dinner.
Sometimes, driving in the car,
the Brahms movement over,
my mother whistles behind her teeth.
Sometimes, in the darkness, she hums.

Second Floor View

Louisa stands at her bedroom window
across the pebbled alley, head framed
between the mullions like the saints at church.
We gesture and mouth words to each other
before full dark sets in.
I imagine her two sisters laughing
as their parents draw baths,
steam rising the way it did over the lake
last spring after the thaw.
I've closed the door so my mother
will think I'm reading just like she is
with a heavy book.

When I was eight, we approached over the city.
The plane seemed to be moving in slow motion
over the bleary shapes of granite towers,
then the more distinct lit windows
of buildings so small I wanted to move them
like red and green pieces in Monopoly.
I could be safe in a city like that.

By now, Louisa has gone to the hallway
and turned off her light.
My mother doesn't know I'm here
waiting, looking out at cars
on the corner of Garfield
or that it has started to rain
so the alley looks like glass,
casting back streetlights,
rain falling on the curbs,
on the lawns, on the roofs
of houses all around.

Sunday Drives

Sundays in the country people sit out the long
afternoon on their porches
watching as a flock of birds,
tender as an apparition, disappears
into the light and the air.

My mother admired this husk of silence,
how they sat comfortable with one another looking,
the herd of Angus defining the field by the creek.

It was then she became so completely relaxed
she would count the houses,
each a reassurance that life could be ordinary
as the dust of the road rose up behind us,
weightless as talcum or soot.

Fortune Fish

Clark buys a paper fish to curl
in the center of his large palm.
He shows me as our spaniel lies dreaming
and the neighbors' porch voices carry
over Stillman's pond where timothy
dries the color of sandstone.

The fish is red and translucent.
It tells Clark his fortune
and he returns it slowly
to its delicate, waxen envelope.

When the neighbors' house catches fire
I am the only one at home.
Around me the rooms of our house
grow quiet and continuous as if
someone had slammed the door, angry.
It happens so fast I cannot answer
any questions but wonder if
the fish said this would happen.

Clark talks to God out of his window.
He says that's where God is,
not in our house, not under our roof.

At night I take out the fish.
If it curls up entirely, I am
full of passion. If it lies still,
I do not have enough love.
Inside the glass lightning rod
I think the moon must be God,
that it is God in the globe on the roof.

When Clark is sent away to school, I still
hear his footsteps pacing the floor upstairs.

Labor well, thy minute particulars.

—William Blake

Learning What My Mother Sees

In Georgia, late summer, farmers are burning
their fields. It is done in a spiral.
One sets it and another follows to damp it out
so what you would see from above
would be a small brilliance getting smaller.
She taught us to make do
so if the next moment brought
what we most feared, we'd be ready.
When the time came for us to leave,
she grew silent, the accumulation
of all she had told us at once,
shocking, the way, after waiting all winter
for the first grass,
its brightness will stun you.

Learning to Write Cursive

In a family, what isn't spoken is what you listen for.
—Joyce Carol Oates

After dark I walk the rutted dirt road the creek
runs beside, neighbors' lights hazy through November air.
I do this so I can be invisible the way an island ferry
moves transparent across the wide ocean.

My mother wrote with her left hand curved
over the letters so the side of her palm
wouldn't smudge what she'd already put down.

From my room across the hall where first light
forms shapes on the green rug, I can see her.
This is what she cares for more than anything,
and I want her to teach me, too,
want a mystery so exalted it has no sound at all.

But in school, with my right hand,
I copy the curly letters
perched above the chalkboard.
I am nothing like her, after all.

Now, it's a month before Christmas
and in the vacant lot next to the video store,
a man sells rugs, transistor radio perched
on his truck's silver hood.
He waits all day but there's never anyone,
his finger tapping out songs on metallic paint.

Tonight I walk, and two cars dim their lights
as tires swish along the stretch of road.
They are going somewhere I hadn't thought of,
night darker once they have passed all the way.

Maybe That's Who I'll Be

The field is ploughed under for fall,
geometric clods the size of your fist.
But this dream really happened, and not so long ago.
My daughter is standing on the end of a diving board.
I'm in line behind her as she peers
through the green water of the pool
so to sit on the balancing end of the board
means I'm part of her decision to jump.
Whole minutes pass still as anything
I can show you right now.
Still as Doric columns.
Stiller than night air.
Then she just steps forward
into the unfathomable water.

One winter I was sledding on the steep hill
next to the National Cathedral
and a boy in my brother's class
went straight into a hemlock.
The ambulance's lights were not
as bright as blood splayed out on rutted snow.
That night I saw a fox crossing
the busy street by the railroad
tracks heading west.
The plane on my way to see the boy,
two decades later, comes down
out of the clouds into the snow
of Michigan a few days before Christmas.
When he meets me his body
smells the way a garden will in spring after thaw.
He draws me a flower,
pointillism, stirring with tiny dots
so you see it the way you can see birds so well in snow,

or the seeds of persimmon, color pocketed
like the one thing you're afraid to tell anyone.

In the airport bathroom, the piped-in song
is "Away in a Manger." For the first time
I think of the singing child loving this new sleeping baby,
such sureness in knowing there are stars in the sky,
someone who might really care after all.
Everything I say here is true. And just now, a man
went back to thank the cook who must have been leaning,
since dawn, over the grease and heat
of his mottled industrial stove.

Person, House, Tree

The only child bears down
on the paper: drawing the hiding places,
every place she might have dreamed of,
the unlit closet she sinks into
beneath stored bags of clothing,
heat from the chimney untraceable and fine as gossamer.
Is there anything else to be said?
Like the very last moments of daylight,
the night will be dark, just like that.
But the house is a drawing, a child's picture.
Outside, dried shells of tulip poplar
hold the snow perfectly. Tree trunks mirror themselves
in the lake. And on the blacktop, children chase their shadows.
Years ago, a friend's mother, a woman I barely knew,
carved an etching of herself trapped behind a window,
the mouth so desperate I could say anything to her afterwards.

The Flat Track

The summer wheat shone purple,
green darners cruised over puddles where,
since June, algae grew in a spreading mosaic
and the girl was convincing.
She'd wanted all summer to breeze
one of the horses, even having smelled it:
dark sweat on her palms where she'd hold
the neck tight, loving the horse.
All summer she'd leaned against the tarred
rails and watched another rider,
afternoon sun hot on her back.
At last, late August,
they put her on the bay mare
and led her across the narrow pasture
whitened with seed-blown dandelion
toward the raked training track, one mile around.

What she didn't know was how,
at this gait, a thoroughbred won't be pulled back
and to tighten the reins only pushes
the horse further out of control.
The girl must have felt a long time pass
and the horse still running, speed below her
on the ground as the hooves blurred together like oil.
She must have stopped counting how many times
around, how many times past the gate where
stable hands stood with blankets to throw at the hooves
until, finally, the mare ran herself lame.

You can tell me otherwise, but it is not until winter
that your shadow will lengthen behind you,
that the angled light will bless your house,
falling at noon on the bright, blue rug.

Fire and the Sun

In the early hours of the morning, in the damp, black streets,
out of worn cardboard, the fruitseller lifts radiant oranges.

Bright-chested pigeons sit fat on the far city roof.
Under the shredded awning, they dip into a hollow of their own.

A boy drags a magnet on a string
its horseshoe shape pulling away what he passes.

From the fourth floor the ground coarsens
against the crucifixes of electric poles.

Do not mistake the colorful swirled sky of hopeful
spring evenings for anything more.

Letter

At least, in this world, I can show you something,
a piece of fruit or a bright jar of buttons,
and it will be what I have said.

Across the road my neighbor
calls his cows home at dusk, call echoing
across the hill with broomsedge, across
the meadow where cornflowers grow
thick this July. Listen——*sookiee whoooo.*
Like the wind his call

is the sound in moon,
sound of children crowding
around a seahorse suspended in shadowy water,

sound of pigeons on the attic roof. Like the wind
he calls them home. Look——just over that hill
they gradually file towards him.

A Study of Gratitude

Last Thanksgiving with my brother
in a bar; it was afternoon
and then it was night and somewhere in the time
between, he told me what had happened,
that because I was younger and went up to bed
there were whole hours I never knew about.
In the half light of the city kitchen
he and my father fought and fought until
a glaze rose high in their chests.
The next day they were civil to each other,
but every night they rehearsed this again,
just the two of them, until the year my father left.
Without understanding this, I have lived remote,
a cloud or a piece of gauze,
something so pale it gives up its form.
I do not know what they fought about
or what they said at the end
of each night that let them give up
and climb the hall stairs to their separate rooms.
But I do understand that this story had a life
long before I had these words.

What I Wanted to Tell You

How, far from here,
mountain laurel open their proud flowers
on Pisgah, waxy leaves grown darker
as summer folds into itself.

How evenings when I walk the path
Hereford have woven through
these woods, ragged daisies growing
alone together, I am bewildered
by the shape of things around me.

How an old man I met knew
it was going to rain when the pin oaks
turned their leaves underneath.

Just now I must wait for the voices
around me to be heard.

What's Alive Inside You

Winter nights I go looking for the whippoorwill
but she's not to be found,
spotted feathers quiet as brackish water,
as cursive letters in a child's handwriting book.

Before the time I could know things
and say them like I am here,
I saw bank swallows swoop into their burrow
along the marsh, one brood, a clutch of five.

I held dark tobacco bunched
from the smoke market floor,
plant cut whole in the field
late October, sixty pounds to a bale.

Lawson has woven his leaves into a hand,
wrapped the biggest one to bind so
once the market bell rings and buyers scatter
these aisles inspecting leaves, smelling for mold,

one will stop for the light
through the vented roof that hits this cluster
restoring it to what is has been
and will be—dazzlingly on fire.

Radiator Heat

In spring, tilled fields stand immaculate, carved
with distinct grooves of plain earth where seed
will wait through the last nights of frost
just as my mother waits: uncertain and alone
upstairs in her sitting room far into morning.
Through the slit of my bedroom door, the hazy shaft
of light and the noise she makes clearing her throat
mirror her suspicion he'll never come home.
Tonight the entire house clangs as cooled water drops
to the basement, copper pipes
singing the pressure of such a falling.
Then, as boiling water rises up,
whistling fills the air, solace shapeless
as a crowd's blur over the radio.
This house is practical, center stairwell,
brick, sensibly set on a side street where cars
sweep up and down the crossroad avenue.
Whenever it rains, headlights spread out
in rays on the wet pavement unrestrained
like splatters of clay on a pottery wheel.
In the morning she'll point to the dogwoods.
See how they look now?
After this rain they are russet,
a color complex enough for fall.

Lucy

Lucy lives behind the house back of the barn,
red oil drums set out to catch the rain.
The afternoon has almost emptied,
light moving in starts over the eastern trees.
She is outside sweeping her dust yard
into perfect swirls, the wings of a night moth.
She does this so that grass won't grow
and snakes can't hide.

All day she has boiled whites, watched the dirt
rise into the scalding wash water, all day
with what is worn next to the skin, hanging
the underwear out brilliant in the July sun.

At times I feel a darkness inside myself,
she tells me, and her voice is so smooth
I feel a cold running in me I have never felt before—
she tells me time will pass faster as I get older,
that I won't want so much anymore.

Mantle of Greens

—for my father

I

You were careful with the card table, angling it
on the oriental, and every ornament wrapped in tissue,
some so grayed it looked like mist.
It must have come from your childhood
bearing its own history of shapes:
pentagons indented in the frail paper.

Outside the window the afternoon
could have blazed red, streaks pawing the sky.
In your partner's office, your chin had dropped
to your chest—what looked to him like a cat nap.
This is the moment I cannot picture.

After you died your sister gave me a whole album:
photographs cataloging how you would angle your body to please—
your arm reaching to feed the Great Dane.
Another, I guess you are thirty, lying with your brother
and sister on a picnic blanket. You're in the center,
hoping to reach them both.
This is what killed you.
Trying to bend in too many ways.

You must have felt you needed to,
small as you were in a family
of statured men, so you moved out
for a woman you didn't love
one July when I was away at camp
as if comfort and routine weren't possible
after all.

These things are boundless and unsheddable.
We go through the motions: every Christmas
spreading spruce and fir on the mantel, the trunk
of ornaments locked in the attic, no tree.
At night I go alone into the living room
with only the blur of the lit globe and see
the feathery shadows of dark evergreen
half covering what was once there.

II

There is a story my mother can tell,
letting go, for the telling, of all the sharp questions.
Every year on your birthday, your parents stood the children
in the doorjamb to measure in pencil where you came to
with your initials lined up, as if to show a landmark of some progress.
You went first to get it over with, precisely lining
the curved back of your oxfords against the baseboard,
your chin and eyes straight ahead.
When Harriet and Sam grew far past the calendar nail
on the adjacent blue wall, you stayed parallel with it.
You were sixteen and still, they measured.

I look through the album—as a very young boy next to your sister,
your hand near hers, no one could hold you up, not even then.

Beside Still Waters

Where earliest light gathers in dense shafts
along the field, I push lettuce into pails
of water to chill them for market.
Next to this dark water grows hemlock
whose limbs wreathe above the shaded stream.
This is the place sorrow comes from,
the time I wanted to tell you,
where the not telling grew into me,
where a tree grows around a cable
where quail ask their bobwhite over and over
filling the air with that plain word.
I know some things by heart.
Listen for psalms in the water
unwavering with mercy.
Above the stubble in the field, sparrows rise
in a rapture. Water is a cold shock,
astonishing and strong and pure.

Photographs of My Mother

Usually she is looking to the side:
at her ankle or a random patch
of grass. And always, no matter who else
is there, she seems removed, complete.

In 1937 a photographer came to the park
and, for a dollar, took pictures of children
on his pony. She looks trapped,
posed aboard the chestnut mare.

In my christening picture she holds me
effortlessly as if we both could rise away like that.

She is always thinking of something else:
how she will imagine this years from now,
or how the salt in the sea comes from rock,
Pacific Ocean larger than all the land in the world.

If you look closely shadows
of the alley trees pour over the smooth
pavement and her hands
are suspended, weightless.

Outwardly, she did what she was supposed to:
married after college, had two children, gave us
the routine we needed. But underneath she lived
with the books she read, certain in her flawless memory.

In this picture she is biting her lower lip.
In this one she is whistling.
In this last, zinnias are bright around her.
She must suspect they will not stay that way.

How My Mother Waited

This evening Lena Wright's hens
wander in her yard, into the cool air
that comes from underneath, from the grass,
and rises through the thicket along the drive.

Because Clark is old enough, we've walked
the mile by ourselves to get a dozen eggs.
I can see us: two children careful in single file,
walnuts from the storm strewn in the gullies.

Most often it was what she didn't say
that was important. Whenever we left like that,
with her permission, she looked at us a long time
silently and then went back upstairs.

What I didn't know was that she'd gone to write down
what we were wearing—the blue of my pants, the white
of Clark's shirt—so if we never came home
she would know exactly how to describe us.

Last Dream Before Waking

We drive past the stone church
where retired men fish like shadows
under the reservoir bridge.
Their arms sweep half circles
as they cast their lures in the still water.
It is winter and the tires ring
against the grooved pavement of the bridge;
and the men who fish here all day,
arriving at first light with full thermoses of coffee,
share long silences that seem, from this distance,
so practiced I imagine they spent their whole
lives hoping for something like this.

Even when we drove together once I was grown,
if we came to a sudden stop,
you would throw your right arm out to brace
me back. Once, soon after I married, a truck
appeared out of nowhere and you did this
as you must have hundreds of times seamlessly.

But in this dream, there is no near accident,
only the hum of the car and the prospect of a day
together. Beside the road, sheer grasses stand,
and steam hovers over the perfect water like moss.
You tell me you have rearranged the room,
set the wing chair closer to the window so evening
light falls on your lap as long as it possibly can.

Old Roads

Tufts of long grass in a straight line
where the bellies of cars packed them down,
look distant and true, sunken in this fertile land,
this safe place we search for and never find.

With two rows of oak, these roads were
the best route to the post office, confession.
So I came to believe that all our journeys,
afternoons in the car pointing at the low,

soft roads, would lead us to one place where
everything uncertain would, at once, be what we wanted.

Metamorphosis

In first grade we rubbed textures
on thin sheets of paper:
the impressions of cinder
block, a white oak leaf, the palm
of Mrs. Lindsten's large hand.
The smell in the hallway was always
the same and words from the
science class came up to us odd
and startling as their teacher explained
eggs, larvae, pupa, adult.
How unlike what we are doing,
as we press firmly with
crayon, how strange to first
be one thing and then another.

Luminescence

Tonight the stars are above cloud, invisible.
They are the brightness under ocean water.
If it were not for what I have been kept from saying,
I would have no words, the darkness coming out of me
like oil as it does out of Stephen who paces
the oriental over and over, paces around
our mother pretending not to notice.

I know this doesn't work.
I know I cannot invent some other truth.
The ocean holds living creatures too frightening
to face: the eel and flat, fast skate.
The ocean also has its own stars
when the light is right.
The ocean's stars are green.

III

Those who dwell, as scientists or laymen, among the beauties and mysteries of the earth, are never alone or weary of life. Whatever the vexations or concerns of their personal lives, their thoughts can find paths that lead to inner contentment. Those who contemplate the beauty of the earth find reserves of strength that will endure as long as life lasts. There is symbolic as well as actual beauty in the migration of the birds, the ebb and flow of the tides, the folded bud ready for the spring. There is something infinitely healing in the repeated refrains of nature—the assurance that dawn comes after night, and spring after the winter.

—Rachel Carson
The Sense of Wonder

What We Watch Behind Glass

At the grocery store the butcher
hauls a side of meat out of the freezer
and cuts it with gloved hands,
sharpened knife lustrous as he grips each piece,
stainless steel counters echoing the light overhead.
As he works, he is whistling behind his teeth.

Last week I watched planes take off at the airport.
From their standstills on the runway they rushed,
one after another, at such speed it was both shocking and exalted.
Light appeared where there was none
before, and particles of dust in the air shimmered
like mica with its delicate, embedded stars.

Because she was so sick
they kept her alone in the room
and studied the monitors from outside.
This was the first night
when they thought she still had a chance.
Four television screens wavered iridescent
through hospital glass, the room
around her stark and impossibly clean.

Names of What We Pass

As we drive by a church
where a funeral has just let out
my daughter wants to know
what they did in the brick building
all dressed so dark.
I point to the sharp-shinned
hawk above, remind her
how earlier we searched for kittens
the feral cat had hidden
far up in the woods
behind the Creasy house.
In architectural blueprints,
a figure is drawn in the doorway
so proportion will be clear.
But I cannot even see
myself, however I am.
In the air I outline letters
so she can see the names
of what we pass, of the meadow we
watched the storm ride over
the barn where the light grew dim.
Across the hall from my childhood
bed there was a leopard woman
in a Depression painting:
shameless dots of her hose
pressed against his soft fur.

Winter's Crèche

That week ice began to form
all the way across the river,
enameled layer from one shore
to the next. Later, cinders
from Lester Morris' chimney sparked
shapeless, fallen leaves until the side
of Flattop Mountain went up in fire.

At night, when you look outside,
you only see yourself.
The thin snow on the ground reflects
what light there is and the whole world
turns back just like that.

My daughter is two and believes
she is hiding when she holds her own
hands in front of her eyes. She calls
to me, or to the room around us, calls
Come find me. Where am I?
If I forget to answer, her voice becomes
impatient and troubled, afraid.

This January on the road to town
one family has kept up their crèche
far past Epiphany. Mary and Joseph
still lean over the manger.
Sheep and cows still graze,
one bright star still floats
resplendent above their heads.

Minuet

This is a sketch of a child
walking down the driveway
away from her home,
each day a little farther,
picking her way accurately
among gravel and rocks
looking back only to make sure
I'm still on the porch
watching her disappear.

Dreams After Her Death

Lately she appears more often:
at the head of a long table like Jesus
or at her own mother's funeral, her dress brown
and proper and world a flooded plain all around.

She came most clearly the summer after her death.
Clark and I have set up the house
for the estate sale, but she is still alive
and says the white Wedgwood can get a good price.

The smell of rain on hot pavement
drifts into the room where we are working,
and the faded carpet holds
indentations from the dining table.

We all know she is about to die.
But it feels like a secret and there is nothing
anyone can say. Come, look at the zinnias:
they are flowers inside of flowers.

Growing Up in Washington

The streets are orderly. They move through
the alphabet starting at the canal where slow
barges carried beaver pelts to the Potomac
to be put on ships for England.

After all the letters, the names start,
first with two-syllabled words and then
three-syllabled ones: Garfield, Hawthorne;
Brandywine, Chesapeake.

Amelia's mother brushed my hair after she gave
typing lessons to Mrs. Pilkington. She said it was beautiful,
thick, the way she'd wanted her own.
Then she let me go for dinner.

In summer we played kick-the-can in the alley
where pebbles jutted from the cracked pavement.
Louisa and her two sisters, all exactly one year and one day
apart, brought cream soda from their father's pantry.

As I tell you this, I can see that it's unremarkable, really.

But when we sold the house last spring after the estate sale,
after my mother died, I could smell something
in the city air, something I loved. And I thought
it had to be written down, as I have here.

Sundays the bells in the tall tower
at the National Cathedral are still rung by hand.
The peal is sweet and flawless and carries
through the neighborhood even in rain.

Columbia Hospital for Women

It was Ash Wednesday, cold and sunny.
After she woke, they brought me to her
so she could prop me on her knees
and look out the fourth floor window
over the rowhouses of northwest Washington.
At night, after the hospital halls dimmed,
she saw lights in houses coming on
one by one, building on themselves
in rapid succession like an arpeggio.

But in this dream my mother is older
than she would be if she were alive, bent
over with a dowager's hump, hair vivid gray.
We're in an auditorium to hear Handel's
Grand Concertos, and our seats are in the back.
I want to make everyone disappear
so she can see straight down to the orchestra
pit where two dozen violin bows
shoot up each time the music rises.

Magic Show

The child nimbly holds a sparkler of light,
share of brightness, like a parcel of land,
so what matters most becomes effortless,
trailing her in the low meadow at dusk.

You can change a person's life
by saying just one thing, just once.

It is the fourth of July, and off in the distance
older children, insistent as shadows,
call for the fireworks to begin.
Who is she that light will stay with her?

A Greek chorus moves together so as to
be believed as one, everything in song.

At home, her mother draws water
into the cast iron tub, holds her hand
under the faucet, still for one brief moment
as she has not let herself be before.

In the field, the fireworks have begun.
But this part of the story you already know.

She takes a hydrangea blossom, the brightest
blue, drapes petals all over the porch
facing Little Flattop Mountain,
and puts on a magic show, lighter than their frailty.

A shadow stays with us when there is light.
See your shadow? See mine?

Blowing Glass

The homeless man
we picked up
at Schoodic Point
hauls everything
he owns in a black plastic
bag on his back.
In the shade
of a fir tree
at the road's end
he sits
as we drive away.

*We should have shown
him the ocean,*
you said.
We should have
taken him closer
to where
he wanted to be.

To shape even
the simplest
form in glass
is a constant fight
against the will
of gravity.
Look at an old window:
how it sags,
how glass is thickest
at the bottom.

Out of the air
shivers a rock dove,

coo coo coo.
Is he cold?

What the Snow Reveals

In the downtown coffee shop two women lean
close to each other across the counter.
The older, whose shift has just ended, sinks
her head into the soft fold of her arms in laughter.
They are friends. You can tell by just hearing them—
the broken talk of having worked side by side for so long.
The older woman's hands remind me of the night nurse
as she wiped the hair from my mother's forehead.
She had a wet washcloth
and would lay it at the top of her brow
as if nothing in that room mattered as much.
I knew then that she understood something I did not,
something about the last hours and how
life moves into death without a start or a cry.

Now the woman walks out to catch the city bus home
where she will sit at her kitchen window looking out
over the winter trees. She thinks the air smells
of soapstone, clean and blue. Over the radio,
a naturalist explains that the snow leopard hides
with its tail in a curtain around its head, spending
most of its life alone, unobserved. The woman dozes
and wakes, safe in the seamless time between the two.

In a lifetime you can only be one person.
You choose without knowing it until one day
you see what you have done.

Reading to the School Group

Here is a picture of a boy in a field.
He's in Sweden and the wood he carries
for fire looks papery and white, like birch.
When the train passes by the library,
all the windows rattle, and the boy
seems suddenly far away.

Ice so thin, he falls through.
Friends throw a rope, but he can't reach it.
They try again and again, frantically,
and the boy is afraid to move
for fear he will come up
in a place the ice won't give,
where it is swollen in a heave
or thickened like on the shade
side of the trough
at the Collins farm.

He is going to drown
in the fragile light of early October.

Country Auction

Someone's bedroom's out here,
set up like it would've been in the house,
headboard carved, wood dark as winter.

A neighbor with thickset hands
and tender eyes guards
the table of tools all day,

feeling the sky turn,
heat building cautiously
over the fields.

Most of us have come
out of a craving
for someone else's life.

So you can see why
when we sold my mother's things
I couldn't be there.

The auctioneer's voice is strong
as if he's sure
of what is coming.

He lifts a pitcher to the light,
pointing to the flower pattern,
how distinctive it is.

Ascension

This time the dream is about sacrifice:
who is willing to give up their life
for another, who will tell the truth
when the house burns down.

Next door is the anatomy classroom
where a cadaver rests
on the formica table. Each day I think
of going to see it, how I'd lift

the sheet back to the face
of someone I've never known,
skin paler than wax
and much more fragile.

My mother was most alone
in the company of others.
She could close herself in
in a way I have never seen

like the homeless woman
who wanders the city
assuming a life that can't be
found in any house.

Right now students perch next to
the replica of a skeleton, counting ribs,
writing down what they've found
as if to report some truth.

If, at last, all things are fire,
look up there:
a hot air balloon hovers mercilessly
over the November field.

Country Burial

She is not afraid of the snow for her household;
For all her household are clothed with scarlet.
—The Book of Proverbs

A pitch cold February and the preacher's voice, rolling louder,
has turned brittle and dry as stubble in the field.
He insists on where she will go. I think of clouds, how they thicken,
of how bees will multiply on the flowers of her grave.
In April bright grass will push through the invisible crease.
People walking will say it is a new grave:
Nellie Hall, married sixty-nine years, her children's
children far from her. Once, on a long afternoon in May,
I watched her husband dig a perfect line of holes
while she dropped a kernel into each,
covering it afterwards with the fine earth.

Now he divides a bale into single bricks for his herd
who come right up to him.
He does this so slowly he seems not to be moving
and I wonder how it would be to move after that,
how everything must look vague, the delicate circles
his cows pace out no more a design to remember for her,
or the bull calf, born into the blizzard, which first got up
onto the half-leg, kneeling, then all the way,
which will not go beyond his thinking but remain
there the way an act of kindness, the man who pulls
his neighbor's truck from the ditch in the dark
or the child who sees his grandfather alone
and sits with him, goes unnoticed, just ends.

The Shadow the House Makes

This sky low with fall,
my neighbor paints *No Trespassing*
on the creosoted fence.
Under the line of spruce:
dense shadow like when the cows
cluster, shifting around the trunks.

He wants the hunters out
but he can't do anything more
or a shed will be burned,
some livestock missing come morning.

Beside me his house's shadow
lies on the ground, exact
but smaller, which is to say, more real,
more like in my dream.

Above it wood smoke streams, silenced,
the way heavy snow curtains a house
and inside all talk is changed.

He says grass doesn't have its strength
until May when the cows stop coming
to his truck parked high on the hill.

Many afternoons I've seen him there
and, from this distance, he looks to be barely moving.

He says before the blight, in spring,
chestnuts, when they bloomed,
looked like snow on the mountain.

The Flower Loves the Water

When the storm passes he hears something.

A bloodhound shifts under the porch
next door where they're never home.

Quieter than that, maybe the swish
of the carp's veil tail in the pond's sweet water.

If only he could become dim as the moths
his mother followed with her eyes
afternoons on the screened-in porch.

He thinks this balanced on the girder at the job site on Grove.

One looks and looks and cannot see.

He swears he can hear the past, standing still,
listening to the sound of the light.

He's wide, wide awake.

Ask what wonder is.

It sends us back to the edge of the sea.

Two Moments with Strangers

The day I walk all ten miles
of the Ridge Road,
I stop to ask for water from a man
whose tended garden blooms
against the chipped metal of his trailer
where his wife shifts about in the heat
praying that a storm will rise
over the near mountains.
The water is sweet and I thank him.
Red poplin curtains wave back
and forth in a fan's path.
Soon, the man promises, *soon*
your baby will be born
and it will be a girl
as you have wished so hard for.

✿

The woman in the waiting room
reading *Newsweek* speaks to me
as I make my appointment.
She says Emma is beautiful
and there is something in her voice I recognize.
When I turn to look at her she is wearing
an onyx necklace like my mother's and a wool
blazer and her eyes are small
and bright and she smells of winter
like my mother and I know that
she has come for this one moment.

Ashwood Dry, Ashwood Green

November makes the length between houses
vast, the swing's chain stiff.
The time it takes to fall asleep
fills with hollow whistles.

We buried my father on a Saturday,
red earth of Appalachia tarnished
and piled in such newness I would not look.

Facing west, I let the afternoon wind blur my eyes.
If I stood still long enough, I'd be sightless.
If I looked straight ahead for years, I'd stop wishing.

There is Such Little Space to Tell You This

1.

In the dark closet at my daughter's school,
the teacher holds a light up to an egg.

Early spring and still cold, grasses beside the creek
copper, cows trundle through the pleated field.

The air pocket inside the egg is the size of a thumb.
And all the chick's parts are formed there.

And far from here, the ocean is silver and blue
and a boat is coming in.

The calendar the children mark off,
days like chores, tells when the chick will be born.

2.

I was buying black cohosh to bring the baby on,
when a woman kept me from it, her eyes true brown.

What was the sky like? The night Garland was born
a stretch of blue covered the neighbor's meadow.

I couldn't see it, of course, but where I drifted
in the hospital room, I was sure it was there.

Then a storm felled so many limbs on the county roads
people had to stop their cars to move them out of the way.

I wish I didn't need words to say what I want to.
I felt the baby move whenever I lay down. Then afterwards,

the echo of a kick, how, on a June day, a window's
mullions remain etched in your eyes after they are closed.

About the Book

Type designer Eric Gill's most popular Roman typeface is Perpetua, which was released by the Monotype Corporation between 1925 and 1932. It first appeared in a limited edition of the book *The Passion of Perpetua and Felicity*, for which the typeface was named. The italic form was originally called Felicity. Perpetua's clean chiseled look recalls Gill's stonecutting work and makes it an excellent text typeface, giving sparkle to long passages of text; the Perpetua capitals have beautiful, classical lines that make this one of the finest display alphabets available.

COVER PAINTING:
"Four Sheep Under the Night Sky"
by John Borden Evans
1999, 21 X 12 acrylic on 100% rag paper
from the collection of Jim and Marianne Welch

Special thanks to Dan Albergotti and M. Gunner Quist.

Design by Robert B. Cumming, Jr.

Charlotte Matthews was born in Washington D. C., and her childhood memories are a prominent feature in a number of her poems. She has always felt a great affinity for the land. Right after college, she lived in a tomato greenhouse and farmed in Vermont.

She is the author of two published chapbooks, *A Kind of Devotion* (Palanquin Press, 2004) and *Biding Time* (Half Moon Bay Press, 2005). Her poems have recently appeared in *Virginia Quarterly Review, Tar River Poetry, Meridian,* and other journals. She is the recipient of numerous awards for both teaching and writing including a fellowship from Brown University and a grant from the Klingenstein Foundation. She teaches at Piedmont Virginia Community College and Johns Hopkins Center for Talented Youth.

She lives with her two children, Emma and Garland, in Crozet, Virginia.

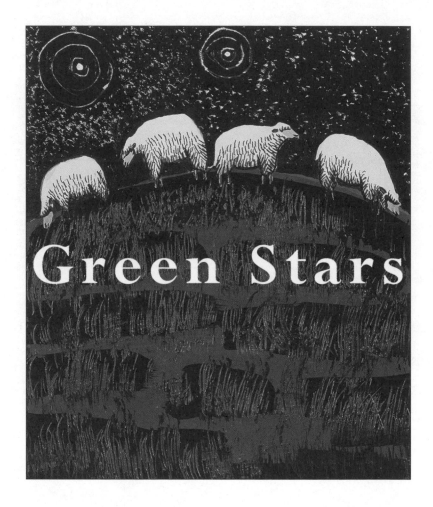

Green Stars